Reinvent U Daily Vitamin

60 day dose to finding your SPARK....Mind, Body, & Spirit

Reinvent U Daily Vitamin

60 day dose to finding your SPARK....Mind, Body, & Spirit

Frances M. Cuesta

© Copyright 2018 Frances M. Cuesta

All rights reserved. This book is protected under the copyright laws of the United States of America. No portion of this book may be reproduced in any form, without the written permission of the publisher. Permission granted on request.

ISBN: 978-0-9991648-9-1

Published by: Unlock Publishing House 6715 Suitland Road Morningside, MD 20746
www.unlockpublishinghouse.com

Unless otherwise indicated, Bible quotations are taken from:
New King James Version (NKJV): Scripture taken from the New King James Version®. Copyright © 1982 by Thomas Nelson. Used by permission. All rights reserved.

New International Version (NIV): Holy Bible, New International Version®, NIV® Copyright ©1973, 1978, 1984, 2011 by Biblica, Inc. ® Used by permission. All rights reserved worldwide.

Living Bible (TLB): The Living Bible copyright © 1971 by Tyndale House Foundation. Used by permission of Tyndale House Publishers Inc., Carol Stream, Illinois 60188. All rights reserved.

Amplified Bible (AMP) Copyright © 2015 by The Lockman Foundation, La Habra, CA 90631. All rights reserved.

Amplified Bible (AMPC): Amplified Classic Edition Copyright © 1954, 1958, 1962, 1964, 1965, 1987 by The Lockman Foundation

Printed in the United States of America May 2018

DEDICATION

This book is dedicated to my two children,
Chenae' & Justin

ACKNOWLEDGEMENTS

A wholesome acknowledgment to my husband, Craig Boone for being my loving strength and support.

Contents

Introduction	11
Day One	15
Day Two	18
Day Three	20
Day Four	22
Day Five	24
Day Six	26
Day Seven	28
Day Eight	30
Day Nine	32
Day Ten	34
Day Eleven	36
Day Twelve	38
Day Thirteen	40
Day Fourteen	42
Day Fifteen	44
Day Sixteen	46
Day Seventeen	48
Day Eighteen	50
Day Nineteen	52
Day Twenty	54
Day Twenty One	56
Day Twenty Two	58

Day Twenty Three 60

Day Twenty Four 63

Day Twenty Five 65

Day Twenty Six 67

Day Twenty Seven 69

Day Twenty Eight 72

Day Twenty Nine 74

Day Thirty 6

Day Thirty One 79

Day Thirty Two 81

Day Thirty Three 83

Day Thirty Four 85

Day Thirty Five 87

Day Thirty Six 89

Day Thirty Seven 91

Day Thirty Eight 93

Day Thirty Nine 95

Day Forty 98

Day Forty One 100

Day Forty Two 102

Day Forty Three 104

Day Forty Four 106

Day Forty Five 108

Day Forty Six 111

Day Forty Seven 113

    Day Forty Eight...115

Day Fifty Nine...117

Day Fifty..119

Day Fifty One 121

Day Fifty Two 123

Day Fifty Three...126

Day Fifty Four...128

Day Fifty Five..130

Day Fifty Six..132

Day Fifty Seven 134

Day Fifty Eight..136

Day Fifty Nine...139

Day Sixty...141

Introduction

Once upon a time, there was a young girl who was full of joyous energy and loved to smile. She was fearless, ambitious, and loved herself despite her differences. People described her as bubbly, happy and sparkly.

Then one day, the dark spell of life and the difficulties it can bring came over the young girl. She began to experience stress and sorrow. She became very good at taking care of others but forgot to take care of herself. She focused more on the distractions of life and got sidetracked from what was important. One day, she kneeled down to pray and asked the Lord, how she lost her spark. The Lord responded and said "my child, you must learn to cultivate your moments and listen to what you are telling yourself. You must learn to trust your struggles and stop people pleasing. Learn to take the limits off and embrace your perfect imperfections. You must shine like a diamond and dream beyond your nightmare. As you are in pursuit of happiness, you must pay attention to who deserves your time and design the life you love and want. Stop carrying what is not yours to carry and challenge yourself to make today your someday. Remember my child, no is not a bad word, and you should never allow others to determine your self-worth. Just be you. Despite your challenges, focus on what you can do now. Get unstuck and stop trying to save people. Be patient and always choose to love and smile".

After many years, now a woman, life still presented its difficulties, and she released the shadow from her past. She was finally tired of feeling tired and living in darkness. She was finally tired of being unhappy. She realized she wanted to live a long and happy life and she had to take ACTION. Through continued prayer, positive thinking, speaking life into her situation and the encouragement of those around her, she learned how to own her power and spark. She learned to create boundaries, she learned to create balance, and she learned to take care and love herself. There she was! She was smiling and laughing again. She finally found her power and her own *SPARK* which had been buried under years of neglect.

Reinvent U Daily Vitamins Definitions

AFFIRMATION:

Affirmations are short, powerful, but simple statements designed to encourage you to have a life filled with positivity. When you see things positively and look for the good in each situation, you have a tendency to remain happy and optimistic. Affirmations are a great way to start your day. It equips you with the tools to handle what may come your way with calmness because you have already affirmed that you are ready for it. Open your eyes and welcome your new day, lie still for a couple of minutes and repeat the affirmation to yourself several times.

DEEP BREATHING:

When you become afraid or upset your breathing becomes shallow. Deep breathing allows you to fill your lungs completely; helping you regulate the flow of oxygen to the body. It allows you to control your lung expansion and heart rate to calm you down. Deep breathing relaxes the muscles and organs, rejuvenates the cells, reduces stress, elevates the mood, builds energy, improves digestion, releases tension and toxins, and strengthens the immune system. In the beginning, deep breathing may feel uneasy or awkward but the more you practice deep breathing, the easier it will become for you.

SCRIPTURE:

Scripture is one of the greatest sources of spiritual food and one of the most precious possessions you own because it is his written message to you. Scripture reading exposes you to the history of the creator's relationship to creation, and that includes you. As you face challenges, pain, sickness, grief and discouragement scripture can restore your hope, peace, and joy. It can reveal when you are heading in the wrong direction and help you make decisions that are aligned with his word.

PRAYER:

Prayer is talking to God; it creates a deeper communion in your heart and soul. Prayer is a natural expression of your relationship with God, and it unleashes power into your life. Prayer allows you to communicate and ask God for what you need. Prayer is also an exercise of faith, knowing and believing that God hears and answers according to his good will and love for you. Praying every day will bring you peace of mind, and you will become more confident about living life to the fullest.

JOURNAL WRITING:

Journal writing is potent and a powerful facilitator of self-discovery which can be used to train our attention and strengthen neural pathways. Daily journal writing forces your mind to become quieter and helps you crystallize your thoughts into written content. Journal writing allows you to create and review your goals, jot down your ideas, and gives you a sense of your own personal growth. Journaling helps to improve both your mental and physical health, reduces stress, relieves anxiety, and boost immune cell activity.

Day One

Reinvent U Daily Vitamin: Taking Action

I remember when I decided to open up my own business; that was such a scary thought. I had a million in one things going through my head on whether or not I had all the tools I needed to start a profitable business (Reinvent U Boot Camps LLC). I quickly realized that everything didn't have to be perfect in order to for me to START. Everything, including ourselves, is a work in progress; you don't have to shoot for perfection at the start. It's not about performance; it's about consistently taking action. Do you know that the manner in which a task is presented to you or the way in which you present it to your brain has a significant impact on how motivated you will be to take action? Therefore, it's very important to break down your task into smaller steps, so it becomes clear and easy to take action.

Mind: By taking positive actions, I bring more positive results into my life.

Body: With one hand on the chest and the other on the belly, take a deep breath in through the nose, ensuring the diaphragm (not the chest) inflates with enough air to create a stretch in the lungs. The goal: Six to 10 deep slow breaths per minute for 10 minutes each day to experience immediate reduction to the heart rate and blood pressure.

Spirit: John 13:17 "Now that you know these things, you will be blessed if you *do* them."

Prayer: Lord help me to grasp the concept of taking action. Lord I want to live as you live in me and through me today and every day. Teach me how to be still so I can hear from you and gain clarity on how to break down my actions so I can continue to walk in my greatness. Amen.

60 day dose to finding your SPARK....Mind, Body, & Spirit

Day Two
Reinvent U Daily Vitamin:
Don't Get Sidetracked

If your focus is not on the right things with the right people, it will get you off track and bring confusion to your life. Don't surrender power to people or situations that are out to steal your focus. Focus can lift every area of your life to new heights. It can bring energy and power to almost anything you do. Don't get sidetracked by people who aren't on track. Be deliberate, be intentional, be focused and let nothing or no one stand in the way of your greatness.

Mind: I focus my mind only on those things which are aligned with my goals.

Body: Inhale for a count of four, then exhale for a count of four; all through the nose, which adds a natural resistance to the breath.

Spirit: Proverbs 4:25 "Let your eyes look directly forward, and your gaze be straight before you."

Prayer: Thank you Lord for the example his life has given to us. Lord, I am standing on faith and prayer to remain focused, deliberate, and intentional. I am thankful for the power you have given me to grow and be great. Amen.

60 day dose to finding your SPARK….Mind, Body, & Spirit

Day Three

Reinvent U Daily Vitamin: LIFE...LIVE it LOVE it!!

Many are not going to support your journey or embrace your story. Many will criticize, question, and disapprove your dreams, passion, and purpose. But you must remain your biggest cheerleader, you know who you are, where you came from, and you know where you are going; so clap for yourself, celebrate yourself and praise yourself. Don't let the judgment of others disrupt your journey or your story. Stop explaining yourself and stop apologizing to folks that will never understand or support U. Keep living, keep loving and keep giving your life the BEST chance it deserves.

Mind: I have much to celebrate about myself and my life.

Body: Take a slow inhale followed by a quick, powerful exhale generated from the lower belly. Take one inhale-exhale (all through the nose) every one to two seconds, for a total of 10 breaths.

Spirit: Psalm 16:11 "You make known to me the path of life; you will fill me with joy in your presence, with eternal pleasures at your right hand."

Prayer: Father I thank you for your love and mercy. Thank you for believing in me when others turned their back on me. You alone define my will and my purpose. Help me and guide me in gaining clarity of who I am in your will so I can continue to give my life the best chance it deserves. Amen.

60 day dose to finding your SPARK....Mind, Body, & Spirit

Day Four

Reinvent U Daily Vitamin: Cultivate Your Moments

Most of us are truly alive only in brief moments. We spend a tremendous amount of our energy on things that take us nowhere, do nothing, and make no difference. I extend an invitation to make today worth remembering. Turn activities into events. Infuse every minute with spontaneous energy, exuberance, and abundance. Begin right now to cultivate special moments as often as you can. Determine what makes you come alive and move in the direction of those heightened experiences. Our life should consist of thirty thousand days, not the same day thirty thousand times.

Mind: I wake up to create moments of being alive.

Body: Make a series of tiny circles with your thumbs or fingertips. Focus on your forehead, temples and jaw muscles. Use your middle fingers to massage the bridge of your nose and work outward over your eyebrows to your temples. Close your eyes and inhale and exhale 10 breaths.

Spirit: 2 Corinthians 9:6 "Now this I say, he who sows sparingly will also reap sparingly, and he who sows bountifully will also reap bountifully."

Prayer: Lord thank you for sacrificing your son so we may live. Thank you for giving me the gift of life and allowing me to cultivate moments that are aligned with your will. Thank you for the courage you have given me to live out my life. Thank you for the overflow of spontaneity, exuberance, and abundance. Amen.

60 day dose to finding your SPARK….Mind, Body, & Spirit

Day Five

Reinvent U Daily Vitamin:
What are you telling yourself?

Do you know the most powerful influence on your life is what you say to yourself? We don't often think about the words we say about ourselves. Yet, those very words have a massive impact on our self-esteem and our self-confidence. Negative self-talk feeds into what we believe we're not versus who we really are. Remember, whatever is expressed is impressed. Whatever you say to yourself is impressed deeply into your subconscious, and it is likely to leave an imprint. Therefore, neutralize those negative thoughts by speaking to yourself positively all the time. There is tremendous power in the word "I AM." Wake up every day and tell yourself: I AM amazing, I AM smart, I AM beautiful, I AM wonderful, I AM successful, I AM confident, I AM determined, and I AM greatness. Press repeat!!

Mind: I AM enough.

Body: Close your eyes and imagine being in your peaceful place. Picture it as vividly as you tap into your five senses. Inhale and exhale 10 breaths.

Spirit: Psalm 84:11 "The Lord is a shield and the source of my strength. He will give me grace and glory. No good thing will he withhold from me because I walk uprightly."

Prayer: Lord thank you for being my great I am. Thank you for a positive mindset. Thank you for reminding me that I am not my past or my mistakes. Thank you for the increased confidence. Thank you for restoring my belief system and thank you for your power. Amen.

60 day dose to finding your SPARK....Mind, Body, & Spirit

Day Six

Reinvent U Daily Vitamin: Trust Your Struggles

Life can be messy when you go through life struggles. Struggles are nothing more than moments that cause you to feel an abundance of negative emotions and can leave you feeling weak and venerable. But despite the mishaps, misfortunes, and struggles that we face as we attempt to evolve, God is so generous; for he gives us a second chance when we wake up each and every morning. And you know what that tells us? It tells us that we must trust our struggles. We must stay awake and committed to the growth required to move beyond the repetitive patterns that no longer suit us; because no matter what our past looks like, no matter how many mistakes we've made along the way, or the number of times we've failed within our journey, our life is still deserving of its best chance.

Mind: My struggles strengthen me.

Body: Take 5 minutes and focus on only one behavior with awareness, Focus on how the air feels on your face while you are still. Inhale and exhale 10 breaths

Spirit: Romans 8:18 "I consider that our present sufferings are not worth comparing with the glory that will be revealed in us."

Prayer: Lord thank you for your strength. Thank you for being my light in moments of darkness. Thank you for being my pillar of hope because my hope is in you. Thank you for trusting me to trust in my struggles. Thank you for renewing my mind and helping me believe that my life deserves its best chance. Amen.

60 day dose to finding your SPARK....Mind, Body, & Spirit

Day Seven

Reinvent U Daily Vitamin:
Laughter is good for the soul!

Do you know that laughing is an effective method to improve and achieve emotional health? We've all heard it before "laughter is good for the soul." Well, it really is, you see laughter reduces feelings of depression, lowers blood pressure, promotes relaxation, reduces stress, increases the oxygen level in our blood, gives us more energy, increases the endorphin activity in our body resulting in a sense of well-being, fights boredom, and increases our enjoyment of life. Laughing does not require the purchase of any special equipment…it's absolutely free. So let's live, love and laugh……BUT laugh a whole a lot more!!

Mind: Laughter fills my soul.

Body: Make an elongated "aeeee" sound as you slowly lift both arms all the way up, and then laugh heartily with your hands pointed to the sky. Imagine that your laughter is coming straight from your heart.

Spirit: Job 8:21 "He will yet fill your mouth with laughter, and your lips with shouting."

Prayer: Lord thank you for helping me see the importance of laughter. Thank you for placing a joyful spirit within me so I can face every challenge and obstacle with hope and excitement. Thank you for bringing laughter into my life and allowing me to share laughter with others. Amen.

60 day dose to finding your SPARK....Mind, Body, & Spirit

Day Eight

Reinvent U Daily Vitamin: Your Time

There are but so many hours in a day, and days in a week and once they're gone, there is simply no way to get them back. No amount of influence, power or money can change the fact that when your time is up, your time is up. Therefore, it is very important for you to use your time wisely and examine where you are allotting the majority of your time. Remember, what we do the majority of the time, affects us the majority of our life. I challenge you to spend time cultivating self, spend time building and birthing your dreams, spend time with people that honor and respect you, spend time fostering relationships that uplift you, spend time with your family, spend time traveling, spend time working on your health, and most importantly spend time praising and honoring God for giving you time.

Mind: My time is valuable.

Body: Stroke in a circle around your eyes with your middle fingers. Stroke firmly and evenly from the bridge of your nose out over your eyebrows, press on your temples and then glide lightly under your eyes, barely touching the skin. Inhale and exhale 10 breaths.

Spirit: Psalm 90:12 "So teach us to number our days, that we may apply our hearts unto wisdom."

Prayer: Lord thank you for giving me the precious gift of time. Reveal to me Lord any area of my life where I am not a good steward of my time. Thank you for placing the dreams in my belly and giving me the time to birth those dreams. Amen.

60 day dose to finding your SPARK….Mind, Body, & Spirit

Day Nine

Reinvent U Daily Vitamin: Forgive Yourself

Forgiving yourself does not mean you get a free pass from trying your best or from taking ownership of your mistake. Forgiving yourself is about softening your own inner conversation when you do miss the mark, and treating yourself with as much kindness, compassion, and love as possible. The next time you make a mistake and feel yourself getting into that familiar cycle of self-criticism, stop. Take a few deep breaths and try a gentler approach. Allow your mistakes to open up your heart and mind to real personal discovery.

Mind: Today I choose to forgive myself.

Body: Take a deep breath and center yourself. As you exhale say out loud "I forgive myself completely. I release the pain, and I release myself. I am free".

Spirit: 1 John 1:9 "If we confess our sins, he is faithful and just to forgive us our sins and to cleanse us from all unrighteousness."

Prayer: Lord thank you for the power of forgiveness. Thank you for wiping my slate clean so that I can live an abundant life. Thank you for removing the shackles and allowing me to be free from bondage and pain from my past mistakes. Thank you for your unconditional love and grace. Amen.

60 day dose to finding your SPARK....Mind, Body, & Spirit

Day Ten

Reinvent U Daily Vitamin: People-Pleasing

People-pleasing requires you to place the needs of others before your own, making it hard to maintain boundaries and balance in your life. Do you want to stop people-pleasing? First, you must understand that you do not need external approval to be a worthy person, second, you must realize that people won't notice, or care as much as you think and lastly, remember the only person you can control is yourself. When you stop people-pleasing, you will notice improvements in the quality of your life.

Mind: I fully approve of who I am.

Body: Close your eyes. Breathe normally through your nose. As you exhale, silently say to yourself "I love myself." Continue for 10 minutes. If your mind wanders, gently remind yourself to think about your breathing and your chosen phrase. Let your breathing become slow and steady.

Spirit: Galatians 1:10 "For am I now seeking the approval of man, or of God? Or am I trying to please man? If I were still trying to please man, I would not be a servant of Christ."

Prayer: Lord I humbly come to you in prayer surrendering my fear of rejection, my negative thoughts, and my need to always please others. Lord, I pray that you give me the spirit of discernment for when to say yes and when to say no. I claim all controlling patterns of people-pleasing are broken, in the name of Jesus. Amen.

60 day dose to finding your SPARK....Mind, Body, & Spirit

Day Eleven

Reinvent U Daily Vitamin: Take Nothing Personally

Do you know that when you take things personally, it's typically a reflection of your own insecurity? In most cases, when you take something personally, you interpret it in a different way than the way it was supposed to be. Taking things personally may cause you to feel inadequate, ashamed, and sometimes angry at yourself which only affects your self-esteem. Know that peoples' behaviors are a reflection of their own issues, not yours. Take the lesson you need to take out of every situation and let the rest go. Your worth depends on U, not on what others say about you or do to you!!

Mind: Today, I abandon my old habits and breathe life into positive ones.

Body: Select a small personal object that makes your heart smile. Focus all your attention on this object as you inhale and exhale slowly and deeply for one to two minutes. While you are doing this exercise, do not allow other thoughts or feelings enter your mind.

Spirit: Galatians 5:1 "For freedom Christ has set us free; stand firm therefore, and do not submit again to a yoke of slavery."

Prayer: Lord help me see and understand things as they truly are rather than I how I interpret them to be. Wrap your arms around me and shield me with your love. Guard my heart and mind and teach me how to love myself the way you love me. Amen.

60 day dose to finding your SPARK....Mind, Body, & Spirit

Day Twelve

Reinvent U Daily Vitamin: Disappointment

We all experience it. Disappointment is an emotional response to an expectation, and when those expectations are not met, we feel disappointed. Someone asked me, "How can I reduce my chances of feeling disappointed?" My response was "By expanding the dimensions of your expectations and living in the moment." We ultimately decide what value we place on any experience. Learning to love your life journey is the best defense against the feeling of disappointment.

Mind: Disappointment has no power over me.

Body: Lie on your back in a comfortable position. Allow your arms to rest at your sides, palms down, on the surface next to you. Raise just the right hand and arm and hold it elevated for 15 seconds. Notice if your forearm feels tight and tense or if the muscles are soft and pliable. Let your hand and arm drop down and relax. Take 10 slow breaths.

Spirit: James 1:12 "Blessed is the one who perseveres under trial because, having stood the test, that person will receive the crown of life that the Lord has promised to those who love him."

Prayer: Lord thank you for giving me the spirit of perseverance and the strength to move past my disappointments. Lord thank you for being my peace and teaching me how to live in the moment. Amen.

60 day dose to finding your SPARK....Mind, Body, & Spirit

Day Thirteen

Reinvent U Daily Vitamin: Stop Watering Dead Plants

It is common for relationships to have difficulties, but there are times when a relationship has reached its dead end with irreparable problems. We must learn to identify when it's time to walk away and stop investing our time and emotions in toxic or dead relationships. If a relationship is inhibiting your growth as a person, then it's time to reexamine yourself and the relationship.

Mind: I choose healthy relationships around me.

Body: Lie in a comfortable position with dim lighting. Play relaxing music. Close your eyes and take 10 slow breaths.

Spirit: 1 Corinthians 15:33 "Do not be deceived: Bad company ruins good morals."

Prayer: Lord surround me with your love, power, and grace. Help me not fear letting go of unhealthy relationships. Help me to trust you for my provision and my protection. Open the eyes of my understanding to see all truth. Amen.

60 day dose to finding your SPARK....Mind, Body, & Spirit

Day Fourteen

Reinvent U Daily Vitamin: Brokenness

When we see mosaic masterpieces, we see beauty, but we often forget the brokenness that masterpiece came from. Do you realize the beauty that could be born out of your own broken pieces? Your "brokenness" does not diminish your value. It makes you human and makes you beautiful. No matter what your broken pieces look like now, there is a future for you, better than you ever expected.

Mind: I love life, and it loves me back.

Body: Find a picture of yourself that makes your heart smile. Focus all your attention on this picture as you inhale and exhale slowly and deeply for one to two minutes.

Spirit: Psalm 34:18 "The LORD is near to the brokenhearted And saves those who are crushed in spirit."

Prayer: Lord teach me to live in peace with you, to make peace with others and more importantly with myself. Give me a fresh vision and allow my brokenness to heal. Amen.

60 day dose to finding your SPARK....Mind, Body, & Spirit

Day Fifteen

Reinvent U Daily Vitamin: Take the Limits Off

Our own life experience teaches us that we have the power of a limitless life by simply being and believing in who we are. We have to take the limits off and open our minds to the possibilities around us and the love within us. You've heard the saying "think outside the box"; I encourage you today to think there is "no box." There are no boundaries to creating pure awesomeness in your life. I challenge you to take the limits off, take the shackles off and create a blueprint for your limitless journey.

Mind: I am deleting all of my limited beliefs.

Body: Take a long, slow breath in through your nose, first filling your lower lungs, then your upper lungs. Hold your breath to the count of "three." Exhale slowly through pursed lips, while you relax the muscles in your face, jaw, shoulders, and stomach.

Spirit: John 14:1-6 "Let not your hearts be troubled. Believe in God; believe also in me. In my Father's house are many rooms. If it were not so, would I have told you that I go to prepare a place for you? And if I go and prepare a place for you, I will come again and will take you to myself, that where I am you may be also. And you know the way to where I am going." Thomas said to him, "Lord, we do not know where you are going. How can we know the way?"

Prayer: Lord I know that I have put limitations on my life. I thank you for blessing me daily and reminding me of those blessings. Father, I claim those limits off by your spirit, and I declare victory over my life in Jesus name. Amen.

60 day dose to finding your SPARK….Mind, Body, & Spirit

Day Sixteen

Reinvent U Daily Vitamin: Be Fearless

It is part of human nature to do things that are safe and don't involve risk. I asked one of my girlfriends to go skydiving with me, and her response was "No way that's too scary." But do you know that skydiving while it looks scary can be so exhilarating. What you might discover is this activity gives us a feeling of accomplishment and increases our base level in confidence. I challenge you today to find something that scares you and do it. Be fearless; it can be the difference between a life of mediocrity or unspeakable happiness and success.

Mind: I breathe faith and let go of fear.

Body: Take a deep, slow breath through your nose for a count of 5 seconds.
Hold the breath for a few 2 seconds, and breathe out slowly through your mouth for another 6 seconds, breathe like you're whistling. Repeat 10 times.

Spirit: John 16:13-14 "However, when He, the Spirit of Truth, has come, He will guide you into all truth; for He will not speak on His own authority, but whatever He hears He will speak, and He will tell you things to come. He will glorify me, for He will take of what is mine and declare it to you."

Prayer: Lord I pray that you give me a heart with no fear. I pray that I will stand boldly on faith believing that no matter what happens I will be victorious. I thank you for every opportunity to be fearless through you. Amen.

60 day dose to finding your SPARK….Mind, Body, & Spirit

Day Seventeen

Reinvent U Daily Vitamin: Choices

The most powerful thing we as humans have is our power of choice. Through our choices, we have the power to change our thinking, our emotions, and our outcomes. Make the decision today to make the best of your life. Choose to enjoy your life no matter what. Choose, right now, to love who you are, to want more, to do more, to give more, and appreciate more.

Mind: The choices I make creates joy my life.

Body: With one hand on the chest and the other on the belly, take a deep breath in through the nose, ensuring the diaphragm (not the chest) inflates with enough air to create a stretch in the lungs. Take six to ten deep slow breaths per minute for 5 minutes.

Spirit: Proverbs 3:5-6 "Trust in the LORD with all your heart, and do not lean on your own understanding. In all your ways acknowledge him, and he will make straight your paths."

Prayer: Lord I pray for the wisdom to guide me through making decisions over my life. Thank you for your grace, mercy, and forgiveness. I pray that as I am faced with making decisions, they are based on your words in Jesus' name. Amen.

60 day dose to finding your SPARK….Mind, Body, & Spirit

Day Eighteen

Reinvent U Daily Vitamin: Help Someone

If you really want to help someone, envision them in a more favorable light than they can see for themselves and allow them to access their own inner strength to reach their fullest potential. Challenge them to own up to who they really are, to walk in their passion and purpose in life, and to feel the joy of personal empowerment and self-confidence.

Mind: I take time to help others.

Body: Hold the right thumb over the right nostril and inhale deeply through the left nostril. At the peak of inhalation, close off the left nostril with the ring finger, and then exhale through the right nostril. Continue the pattern, inhaling through the right nostril, closing it off with the right thumb, and exhaling through the left nostril.

Spirit: Hebrew 6:10 "God is not unjust; he will not forget your work and the love you have shown him as you have helped his people and continue to help them."

Prayer: Lord guide me and show me the way to help those who you place before me. I pray that you heal those that are hurting, provide for those in need, and uplift those that are discouraged. I pray that you open my eyes and make me aware of the opportunities I have to bless others in need. May your will be done in Jesus' name. Amen.

60 day dose to finding your SPARK….Mind, Body, & Spirit

Day Nineteen

Reinvent U Daily Vitamin: Perfect Imperfections

None of us are perfect. But there are times we feel bad for not being perfect. Guess what? I am not perfect, and I will never be perfect. But as long as I have the breath of life, I will choose to be the best me I can ever be. I celebrate my wins no matter how small. I embrace my journey for growth and accept my flaws as an intrigued accessory to who I am. I love me for the me that I am and more importantly, I am proud of my perfect imperfections.

Mind: I love me and my perfect imperfections.

Body: Take a deep breath while focusing on pleasant, positive images to replace any negative thoughts.

Spirit: 1 John 1:9 "If we confess our sins, he is faithful and just to forgive us our sins and to cleanse us from all unrighteousness."

Prayer: Lord I pray that I can be more compassionate and forgiving as I continue to experience the fullness and beauty of life. I pray that I continue to see and embrace my beauty and my perfect imperfections. Thank you for teaching me how to feel for myself and others. Thank you for the peace and harmony in my life. Amen.

60 day dose to finding your SPARK....Mind, Body, & Spirit

Day Twenty

Reinvent U Daily Vitamin: Shine Bright Like a Diamond

Have you ever blocked out your worthiness by choosing to believe you don't have any? Here is a fundamental fact, as long as you believe yourself to be unworthy; you'll never be able to manifest evidence of your worthiness. It really doesn't matter how others see; it's how you see yourself. You were handcrafted to be you, and you are here to shine and illuminate your beauty on this earth. Stop hiding in the dark and shadows and remember you were "fearfully and wonderfully made." Go on now and shine bright like a diamond and step into your light of power, passion, and purpose.

Mind: I shine like bright like a diamond.

Body: With relaxed shoulders take a normal breath for about two counts then pucker your lips up and exhale for four counts. Repeat four times.

Spirit: Isaiah 41:10 "Fear not, for I am with you; be not dismayed, for I am Your God; I will strengthen you, I will help you, I will uphold you with My righteous right hand."

Prayer: Lord I know that you are my rock and my fortress and in you I can find comfort, strength, and the ability to shine like a diamond. Help me to embrace anything that comes my way as an opportunity to see you at work. Thank you for your love, favor, and mercy over my life. Amen.

60 day dose to finding your SPARK....Mind, Body, & Spirit

Day Twenty-One

Reinvent U Boot Camps: When It Rains It Pours

I think we have all heard and can relate to the saying "when it rains it pours." It can feel like you have been singled out to receive more than your share of hardships. Use this opportunity to upgrade rather than repair. We can't always fix what's broken. We can't always use old parts to fix what's broken. Every season has an end if you have to rebuild some aspects of your life; you will probably do it better and faster with newer and upgraded parts.

Mind: I choose to rebuild with upgraded parts.

Body: Take a deep breath and inhale for a count of four, then exhale for a count of four. All through the nose, which adds a natural resistance to the breath.

Spirit: Revelation 21:5 "Behold, I am making all things new."

Prayer: Lord you are my shield, my strength, and strong tower. Teach me how to anchor myself in the moments that I need to upgrade, rather than repair. Show me what parts to use to rebuild the broken areas of my life. I pray that you will be with me as I continue this journey called life. Amen.

60 day dose to finding your SPARK....Mind, Body, & Spirit

Day Twenty-Two

Reinvent U Daily Vitamin: Dreaming Beyond the Nightmare

Will there be dreams and endeavors you'll fail at? Darn right. Will it be stressful and make you second-guess yourself? Absolutely, but you don't stop dreaming just because you had a nightmare. Dreams provide nourishment for the soul. Keep dreaming despite the nightmare, despite the failure, despite the frustration, despite the challenges, despite the mistakes; with each lesson, you'll adjust your path and keep going toward the dream until eventually, you'll arrive at your destination. Be strong, stay positive, and keep dreaming!!

Mind: I will live beyond my nightmares.

Body: Relax each muscle group for two to three seconds each. Start with the feet and toes, then move up to the knees, thighs, glutes, chest, arms, hands, neck, jaw, and eyes, all while maintaining deep, slow breaths.

Spirit: Daniel 2:19 "During the night the mystery was revealed to Daniel in a vision. Then Daniel praised the God of heaven."

Prayer: Lord thank you for the dreams that build my faith. Father, I pray that I will not answer to my nightmares but answer to my dreams. I pray that I will let go of whatever is holding me back from reaching my full potential. Amen.

60 day dose to finding your SPARK….Mind, Body, & Spirit

Day Twenty-Three

Reinvent U Daily Vitamin: The "F" Word

Thomas Edison attempted 1,000 times before he invented the longer-lasting light bulb. He never looked at his prior efforts as failures because he learned what not to do, and gained from the benefit of his past experiences. Failure has the power of transformation to help change our lives for the better. Failure gives us the opportunities for self-discovery, and it will teach us the value of hard work and effort. Learn, like Edison, from your one thousand and one failures, and march along your path with a sense of invincibility.

Mind: I release my failures.

Body: Hold the right thumb over the right nostril and inhale deeply through the left nostril. At the peak of inhalation, close off the left nostril with the ring finger, and then exhale through the right nostril. Continue the pattern, inhaling through the right nostril, closing it off with the right thumb, and exhaling through the left nostril.

Spirit: 2 Corinthians 9-10 "But he said to me, "My grace is sufficient for you, for my power is made perfect in weakness." Therefore I will boast all the more gladly of my weaknesses, so that the power of Christ may rest upon me. For the sake of Christ, then, I am content with weaknesses, insults, hardships, persecutions, and calamities. For when I am weak, then I am strong."

Prayer: Lord, help me let go of my fear of failure. Allow me to live a life with boldness. I claim a life filled with peace, success, and excellence. I rebuke Satan as he attempts to hold me back from achieving greatness. But I know that as long as I stand on faith and on your word I shall live fearlessly. Amen.

60 day dose to finding your SPARK….Mind, Body, & Spirit

Day Twenty-Four

Reinvent U Daily Vitamin: Be Grateful

Too often we assume someone is happy because we see them driving fancy cars, working high paying jobs, dressed in fine clothing, or living in a big, beautiful home. We assume if only we had those nice things in our own life, or had that much money, then, we'd be happy too. But the truth is, happiness is only found when our hearts can be GRATEFUL for all the things God has blessed us with, no matter how small or insignificant they may seem to us. Being grateful brings more abundance and happiness into our life. What are you grateful for?

Mind: I have a grateful heart for everything I have and don't have in my life.

Body: Gently and slowly inhale a normal amount of air through your nose, filling only your lower lungs. (Your stomach will expand while your upper chest remains still.) Exhale easily. Continue this gentle breathing pattern with a relaxed attitude, concentrating on filling only the lower lungs.

Spirit: 1 Thessalonians 5:18 "Give thanks in all circumstances; for this is the will of God in Christ Jesus for you."

Prayer: Lord teach me to be grateful in all seasons of my life. Convict me whenever I complain or compare my life to others. Father, continue to teach me the power of gratitude in all that I do and all that I am. Amen.

60 day dose to finding your SPARK....Mind, Body, & Spirit

Day Twenty-Five

Reinvent U Daily Vitamin: In Pursuit of Happiness

If you want to be happy or happier, make happiness and enjoying life your priority. Learn how happiness works and start building self-happiness. If you don't make happiness a personal priority, happiness will only appear by accident or as an afterthought. Your life is too short for that. You complete yourself; aim for your happiness, own your happiness and become your happiness.

Mind: I am happy.

Body: Begin with a long, slow inhale, followed by a quick, powerful exhale generated from the lower belly. Once comfortable with the contraction, up the pace to one inhale-exhale (all through the nose) every one to two seconds for a total of 10 breaths.

Spirit: Psalm 37:4 "Take delight in the LORD, and he will give you the desires of your heart."

Prayer: Lord thank you for giving me a cheerful heart. Thank you for helping me prioritize my happiness. Thank you for being my source of light in my moments of darkness. Thank you for placing the right people in my life that not only bring me happiness but keep me grounded with a positive smile and an encouraging word. I pray, daily, that my happiness lifts me and those around me. Amen.

60 day dose to finding your SPARK….Mind, Body, & Spirit

Day Twenty-Six

Reinvent U Daily Vitamin: Who Deserves Your Time?

We've heard it before, "time is a precious thing to waste." So why waste your precious time around people who devalue you, dishonor your gift, and try to deter you from your greatness. Always remember, you are influenced by those you spend time with, so you must choose your influences wisely. Who is deserving of your time? People who empower you; people who are improving themselves, people who bring happiness, laughter, passion, honesty, love, trust and hope into your world. Take inventory and begin filling your life with amazing people who are deserving of your time.

Mind: I deserve to have people in my space that deserve my time.

Body: Take a long, slow breath in through your nose, first filling your lower lungs, then your upper lungs. Hold your breath to the count of "three." Exhale slowly through pursed lips, while you relax the muscles in your face, jaw, shoulders, and stomach.

Spirit: Colossians 3:17 "And whatever you do, in word or deed, do everything in the name of the Lord Jesus, giving thanks to God the Father through him."

Prayer: Lord I thank you for being a God who deserves all praises. Thank you for the spirit of discernment and showing me who does not deserve my time. Thank you for placing the right people in my life that bring me happiness, laughter, passion, honesty, love, trust, and hope. Amen.

60 day dose to finding your SPARK….Mind, Body, & Spirit

Day Twenty-Seven

Reinvent U Daily Vitamin: Critics With No Credentials

Don't let the criticism of others hold you back from pursuing your purpose. People around you will find a reason to project their insecurities, their negativity, and their fears onto you and your life. Remember, the people who criticize most usually do not have the knowledge or credentials in the area they choose to criticize you in. Therefore, don't give people permission to vote on how you should live your life or allow the opinions or criticism of others to deter you from your God-given purpose. It's your life...live it and love it!!

Mind: The criticism of others will not dim my light

Body: Take a long, deep breath and exhale it slowly while saying the word "relax" silently. Close your eyes. Let yourself take ten natural, easy breaths. Countdown with each exhale, starting with "ten." This time, while you are breathing comfortably, notice any tensions, perhaps in your jaw or forehead or stomach. Imagine those tensions loosening. When you reach "one," open your eyes again.

Spirit: Matthew 7:1-5 "Judge not, that you be not judged. For with the judgment you pronounce you will be judged, and with the measure you use it will be measured to you. Why do you see the speck that is in your brother's eye, but do not notice the log that is in your own eye? Or how can you say to your brother, 'Let me take the speck out of your eye,' when there is the log in your own eye? You hypocrite, first take the log out of your own eye, and then you will see clearly to take the speck out of your brother's eye."

Prayer: Lord I humbly pray and forgive those who have criticized me. You are the Judge of their heart and mine. I release them over to you, and I pray you continue to pour your grace and mercy over my life. Amen.

60 day dose to finding your SPARK....Mind, Body, & Spirit

Day Twenty-Eight

Reinvent U Daily Vitamin: Design the Life You Love

It can be quite overwhelming at times to live in this world where everybody expects something from you. And if you don't know who you really are, chances are, you will run around like a mad person trying to make everybody happy and making yourself very unhappy. Know who you are and what you value most. If you know yourself well, then the quality of life is easier for you to define. Happiness is about designing the life you love and living your definition of quality of life.

Mind: I design the life I live and the life I love

Body: Inhale for a count of four, and then exhale for a count of four all through the nose, which adds a natural resistance to the breath.

Spirit: Job 33:4 The Spirit of God has made me, and the breath of the Almighty gives me life.

Prayer: Lord thank you for being the designer of my life. Thank you for showing me who I am through you. Thank you for being my anchor of love so I can continue to create a life of happiness. Amen.

60 day dose to finding your SPARK....Mind, Body, & Spirit

Day Twenty-Nine

Reinvent U Daily Vitamin: Pass the Glitter

When you support someone else's success, it ultimately leads to more success for you. The success of one person does not minimize your own success. Let's learn to compliment, encourage, empower, share, uplift and support one another. We are such powerful beings and can accomplish so much more when we support each other. Now pass that glitter.

Mind: I support the success of others.

Body: Gently close your eyes, shift awareness from the external world to your physical space and breathe. After a few rounds of organic breathing, begin extending the length of your inhales counting to six, and your exhales to six.

Spirit: Hebrew 13:16 "And do not forget to do good and to share with others, for with such sacrifices God is pleased."

Prayer: Lord allow me to support others with a joyful heart. I pray that I can continue to support those around me with compassion, and tenderness, never diminishing the worth and success of another. Amen.

60 day dose to finding your SPARK....Mind, Body, & Spirit

Day Thirty

Reinvent U Daily Vitamin: Loving Self Despite....

We have all had someone say something that does not reflect who we truly are, but sometimes we give it so much power that we allow it to define us. Don't lose sight of who you truly are and the unique qualities you've built within yourself. In life, we will meet people along the way who will attempt to tear us down and break our spirit. Love yourself enough to believe that you are limitless, beautiful, intelligent, confident, assertive, creative, passionate, courageous, determined, fearless, charming, electrifying, humorous, happy, intuitive, incredible, marvelous, remarkable, and successful. People can only take from you what you are willing to surrender. Don't let others dictate who you are but more importantly where you are going.

Mind: I have an overflow of self-love.

Body: With sealed lips, start to breathe in and out through your nose very slowly. With each inhale, breathe deeply into your lungs and pause when you've reached the top of the breath. As you exhale, gently constrict the back of your throat and slowly release the air out of your lungs. On your inhales, you'll expand your chest and lungs, and on the exhales you'll press air outward from your navel up to the throat and out the nose. Both inhales and exhales should be longer and deeper than your normal breath.

Spirit: Proverbs 4:23 Keep your heart with all vigilance, for from it flow the springs of life.

Prayer: Lord thank you for loving me when I fail to love myself. Thank you for seeing the best in me when others see the worst in me. Help me to love the person you created me to be, not who others want to see. Amen.

60 day dose to finding your SPARK....Mind, Body, & Spirit

Day Thirty-One

Reinvent U Daily Vitamin: Not Yours to Carry

Have you ever noticed how much time you spend solving other people's problems? It can be tiring and draining being that one friend or family member everyone goes to for relief of daily dramas. The real question is how much of other people's problems do you carry? Remember this, when someone shares his or her problems with you; it is not always an invitation to help the person problem-solve. You can still be that great and loyal friend, parent, partner, family member, etc., without fixating on someone else's life and trying to carry what was never yours to carry.

Mind: I release what's not mine to carry

Body: Inhale a deep breath, pause for a moment, holding your breath. If you're counting with your breath, stay for about two counts, and then slowly exhale all the air out through the nose. At the end of your exhale, keeping your navel pressed against your spine, hold the breath out for two counts.

Spirit: Galatians 6:5 for each one should carry their own load.

Prayer: Lord I pray that you help me have clear parameters on what is not mine to carry. Allow me to set boundaries, so I am protected. Show me, Father God, how to be still in your word, so I know when to move and what to say. Amen.

60 day dose to finding your SPARK....Mind, Body, & Spirit

Day Thirty-Two

Reinvent U Daily Vitamin: Modify or Magnify

You are the captain of your life; you decide exactly what it means to be successful. Success is not coincidence or luck; it's an intentional action. What are you doing right now to create success? You can choose to modify your dreams or magnify your success. I challenge you to own success; want it, believe it, feel it, see it, and taste it. Now proceed as if success is inevitable.

Mind: I believe in myself and my ability to magnify my success.

Body: Gently close your eyes, shift awareness from the external world to your physical space and breathe. After a few rounds of organic breathing, begin extending the length of your inhales counting to six, and your exhales to six. Repeat for 8 rounds or so, then releasing your counting. With a clearer mind, begin to focus on your end "success" goal. Visualize what it would feel like achieving that goal, what you would be doing now in that moment once you are there, and what thoughts are you telling yourself, having achieved that result. Continue this extended breath and visualization for 5-10 minutes.

Spirit: Jeremiah 29:11 "For I know the plans I have for you," declares the LORD, plans to prosper you and not to harm you, plans to give you hope and a future."

Prayer: Lord thank you for giving me vision and purpose. I pray that you enlarge my territory and be with me every step of the way. Allow me to humbly magnify my success and show me how to give of my best. Amen.

60 day dose to finding your SPARK....Mind, Body, & Spirit

Day Thirty-Three

Reinvent U Daily Vitamin: Practice for Growth

We must trust that life is giving us exactly what we need practice in. Our challenges, struggles, and experiences make us stronger and wiser. Our today challenges are merely our practice sessions in order for our future to be brighter and purposeful. Do not be scared of the challenges of life; our challenges make us our own hero.

Mind: My challenges bring out the best in me.

Body: Close your right nostril with your thumb and inhale steadily through the left nostril. Hold the breath for a brief moment at the top. Now, close your left nostril with your ring finger, release your thumb and exhale through the right side. Keeping your ring finger on the left nostril, inhale through the right. Retain the breath for a moment; close the right nostril, release your ring finger and breathe out through the left.

Spirit: Philippians 4:6 "Do not be anxious about anything, but in everything by prayer and supplication with thanksgiving let your requests be made known to God."

Prayer: Lord I surrender myself to you. I open my heart and my soul ready to depend on you for guidance and strength. Father allow me to process the challenges that come my way as a practice sessions for my future. As hard times come my way help me to stand by faith and not by sight. Amen.

60 day dose to finding your SPARK....Mind, Body, & Spirit

Day Thirty-Four

Reinvent U Daily Vitamin: Inspect What We Expect

Experience has the potential to be our very best teacher, and it plays a vital role in the many valuable lessons we gain from life. Many of us go through life repeating the same mistakes over and over again. Therefore, it is so important that we continuously inspect, breakdown, and measure the RESULTS of our past actions to gain a better understating of where we are versus where we want to be. Remember, we must inspect what we expect from ourselves and others.

Mind: I value the lessons and embrace the results.

Body: Place a palm on your abdomen and breathe comfortably for a few moments, noticing the quality of your breath. Gradually begin to make your breathing as relaxed and smooth as possible, introducing a slight pause after each inhale and exhale breath.

Spirit: Philippians 3:13 "Brothers, I do not consider that I have made it my own. But one thing I do: forgetting what lies behind and straining forward to what lies ahead,"

Prayer: Father thank you for the valuable lessons I have gained from life. Thank you for providing me with the tools to inspect what I expect. Thank you for your shining light as I move forward in the pursuit of my goals with renewed focus and commitment. Amen.

60 day dose to finding your SPARK….Mind, Body, & Spirit

Day Thirty-Five

Reinvent U Daily Vitamin: Challenge Yourself

By challenging yourself, you grow as a person, and you learn to trust yourself more. It's time to challenge yourself to greatness, dig deep to find your passion, your gifts, and your power. Get out of your comfort zone, meet new people, travel to new places, start exercising, aim higher in your career, become an entrepreneur. Whatever you do, don't think small, don't hold back, pull out all the stops to unleash your potential. You are unstoppable!!

Mind: I embrace a new perspective of challenging self.

Body: Open the mouth slightly with your tongue just behind the teeth. Inhale slowly through the space between the upper and lower teeth, letting the air wash over your tongue as you raise your chin toward the ceiling. At the end of the inhalation, close the mouth and exhale through the nostrils as you slowly lower your chin back to neutral. Repeat for 8 to 12 breaths.

Spirit: Psalm 19:14 "Let the words of my mouth and the meditation of my heart be acceptable in your sight, O LORD, my rock and my redeemer."

Prayer: Lord thank you for teaching me how to embrace and use my gifts, skills, and talents. Continue to stretch me, continue to take me out of my comfort zone, and continue to challenge me to be greater and better. Amen.

60 day dose to finding your SPARK….Mind, Body, & Spirit

Day Thirty-Six

Reinvent U Daily Vitamin: Stress to Serenity

Stress has proven to be a direct cause of increased physical, mental, and emotional disorders. When we internalize small amounts of unresolved stress, over time, it can have drastic effects on our whole being. Therefore, it is very important that we pay attention to the more relaxed side of life. I challenge you to take a closer look at your life and make a choice to take the necessary steps to lower, manage, and resolve the causes of your stress. This may require you to remove people, things, and behaviors that are not producing positive stress-free outcomes in your life. Don't let stress consume you; remember life was meant to be enjoyed.

Mind: I live a balanced and peaceful life.

Body: Place a palm on the abdomen and take a few relaxed breaths, feeling the abdomen expand on the inhalation and gently contract on the exhalation. With your palm on your abdomen, mentally count the length of each inhalation and exhalation for several more breaths.

Spirit: John 14:27 "Peace I leave with you; my peace I give you. I do not give to you as the world gives. Do not let your hearts be troubled and do not be afraid."

Prayer: Lord thank you for being my pillar of peace. Allow me to remove the people and behaviors that create stress in life. Lord, you said I can cast my cares on you. I release my stress and receive calmness and serenity in my life. Amen.

60 day dose to finding your SPARK....Mind, Body, & Spirit

Day Thirty-Seven

Reinvent U Daily Vitamin: Become SUCCESS

We've all heard the term "you can achieve whatever the mind can conceive," do you believe it? Being successful is not something that just falls into your lap. You have to first adopt a successful mindset and then take action. Your mental attitude determines your success. When your thoughts, beliefs, and feelings are parallel with your purpose and values, your life will change accordingly. Therefore, I challenge you to develop a mindset for success and act in accordance with it and just watch success happen.

Mind: I am a success.

Body: Inhale and exhale as you normally do and then hold your breath. Time the number of seconds you are able to hold before experiencing discomfort. Begin breathing again in the same rhythm you were prior to counting.

Spirit: Philippians 4:23 "I can do all things through him who strengthens me."

Prayer: Lord open my mind and my heart so that I can develop a mindset for success. Thank you for getting me excited about your plans for me and preparing me for growth. Thank you for the overflow of success pouring into my life. Amen.

60 day dose to finding your SPARK....Mind, Body, & Spirit

Day Thirty-Eight

Reinvent U Daily Vitamin: Make Today Your Someday

We are responsible for creating the changes in our life that will produce the outcomes we expect. If we choose to do nothing, then our situation will reflect such. Wanting to change is not enough. You must make a choice to change and then apply the necessary actions to create the change. You have an enormous amount of power to control the QUALITY of your life through your choices. Today, make a choice to have the life you want and allow your choices to cultivate greatness. Make TODAY your someday.

Mind: The changes I make improve the quality of my life.

Body: Lie comfortably with your eyes closed. Breathe through your nose rather than your mouth if that is comfortable for you. Deliberately slow your breathing down. Breathe in to a count of four. Pause for a moment and breathe out to a count of four. Pause and repeat.

Spirit: Hebrew 6:19 "We have this hope as an anchor for the soul, firm and secure. It enters the inner sanctuary behind the curtain,"

Prayer: Father allow me to have the courage to change my life for the better. Allow all my burdens to be risen up to you as I know that you will see me through. Bless me with love, strength, wisdom, health, courage, forgiveness, and a willingness to learn so I can make today my someday. Amen.

60 day dose to finding your SPARK….Mind, Body, & Spirit

Day Thirty-Nine

Reinvent U Daily Vitamin: Difficult People

We have all come across difficult people in our lives who criticize, insult, judge, belittle, gossip, etc. We can't control how they act, but we can control how we react to them. Life is too precious to be upset or offended by others. We have to use every precious time on this earth on things and people that really matter. Make time for people that fill your life with peace, joy, and happiness. If they are not filling your space with positivity, then it's time to re-assess, re-shift and re-assign.

Mind: I re-assess, re-shift and re-assign difficult people in my life.

Body: Take a very deep breath in with your mouth open; fill your lungs up. Hold your breath. While holding your breath, tense muscles all over your body as tense as you can face, fingers, toes, shoulders, stomach, butt, legs etc. without injuring yourself (if you have a known issue go easy on that part of your body) Count 5-10 seconds while holding your breath and keeping all muscles tense. Then relax everything, let go of all the tension in your muscles and slowly let your breath out.

Spirit: Proverbs 22:24 "Make no friendship with a man given to anger, nor go with a wrathful man,"

Prayer: Father thank you for loving me beyond my faults and loving me unconditionally. Thank you for giving me a space of peace, joy, and happiness. Thank you for the spirit of discernment and for showing me how to respond to the difficult people in my life. Thank you for the re-shifting and reassignment. Amen.

60 day dose to finding your SPARK....Mind, Body, & Spirit

Day Forty

Reinvent U Daily Vitamin: "NO" is Not a BAD Word

I remember years ago going through a period in my life where I struggled with saying "NO" to others. My life reached a point of chaos and left me feeling overwhelmed and stressed. I knew I had to create boundaries, I knew I had to start saying no, and I knew I was the problem but I knew I was also the solution. Life changed when the "N" word stopped being a bad word. I stopped feeling obligated to other people and started making "me" a priority. Many were disappointed, but I was at a place of peace. Saying "No" is not a bad word and we are not being selfish or entitled. We're just doing what's necessary to nourish that part of us that feeds our soul.

Mind: I set firm boundaries with those around me.

Body: Take a deep breath into your lower belly (not your chest) and feel your abdomen expand with air. Hold this for a few seconds and then release. Notice your belly rising and falling, and the air coming in and out a few times. Imagine the air filling up your abdomen, and then traveling out your airways, over and over. Continue to do this for a few minutes, focusing your mind back to your body and the breath coming in and out.

Spirit: 2 Timothy 1:7 "For God gave us a spirit not of fear but of power and love and self-control."

Prayer: Lord I pray that you continue to show me how and when to say "no." I pray for strength and guidance as I am placed in situations to create boundaries in my life. Teach me, Father, to obey your word and listen to your wisdom so that I can have peace of mind. Amen.

60 day dose to finding your SPARK....Mind, Body, & Spirit

Day Forty-One

Reinvent U Daily Vitamin: UPGRADE

When your computer is running slow, or it's not working to your satisfaction because it's old, you may consider giving the computer an upgrade. It may be a major system upgrade or a simple program upgrade. Nonetheless, the upgrade allows your computer to perform better and faster. Our lives are very similar; we can't grow using our old ways, using our old thinking, or old behaviors. We must undergo an internal upgrade of our operating systems so we can achieve personal growth. When was the last time you upgraded your internal drive?

Mind: I override negative behaviors through my upgraded internal drive.

Body: Lie down and close your eyes. Start by taking an exaggerated breath: a deep inhale through your nostrils (3 seconds), hold your breath (2 seconds), and a long exhale through your mouth (4 seconds).

Spirit: Ephesians 4:22-24 To put off your old self, which belongs to your former manner of life and is corrupt through deceitful desires, and to be renewed in the spirit of your minds, and to put on the new self, created after the likeness of God in true righteousness and holiness.

Prayer: Lord thank you for what you have allowed in my life. I pray that you would keep my footsteps firm and on solid ground, helping me to be consistent and faithful. Thank you for giving me the tools to make all things new. Thank you for the upgrade and thank you for the newness in my internal drive. Amen.

60 day dose to finding your SPARK….Mind, Body, & Spirit

Day Forty-Two

Reinvent U Daily Vitamin: Plan for ACTION

Planning is very important when you want to create a specific outcome. However, planning alone does not create the outcome…it's planning with action. A well thought out plan of action remarkably increases the chances that the action you take will produce the result you want. So remember that your plan requires action and your action requires a plan!! Therefore, make sure you have a Plan for ACTION!!

Mind: My plans become real with focused intentions and inspired action steps.

Body: Inhale and exhale rapidly through your nose, keeping your mouth closed but relaxed. Your breaths in and out should be equal in duration, but as short as possible. Breathe normally after each cycle.

Spirit: James 4:17 "So whoever knows the right thing to do and fails to do it, for him it is sin."

Prayer: Lord give me the power to be obedient to your word. I pray that when the devils tries to silence my plan for action that your voice speaks louder and stronger in my heart and mind. Lord remove all obstacles and clear the way so that I can plan, create, and take action. Amen.

60 day dose to finding your SPARK….Mind, Body, & Spirit

Day Forty-Three

Reinvent U Daily Vitamin: Pat Yourself on the Back

There is nothing wrong with patting yourself on the back. When you work hard on a project or goal, find a way to reward yourself. It is not egotistical to give yourself acknowledgment; it serves as reassurance to self. It's great when others validate you, but it's even greater when you have the ability to validate yourself and your accomplishments. Feel proud!!

Mind: I am proud of me.

Body: Exhale completely through your mouth, making a whoosh sound. Close your mouth and inhale quietly through your nose to a mental count of four. Hold your breath for a count of seven. Exhale completely through your mouth, making a whoosh sound to a count of eight.

Spirit: Philippians 4:8 "Finally, brothers and sisters, whatever is true, whatever is noble, whatever is right, whatever is pure, whatever is lovely, whatever is admirable—if anything is excellent or praiseworthy—think about such things."

Prayer: Lord with you all things are possible. I thank you for trusting and believing in me. Thank you for the visions and dreams you have paced in my belly. Thank you for allowing me to humbly validate and acknowledge all of my blessings and accomplishments. Father, I pray I continue to stay focused and steadfast to do your will. Amen.

60 day dose to finding your SPARK....Mind, Body, & Spirit

Day Forty-Four

Reinvent U Daily Vitamin: Power of Association

There is unbelievable power in association. Make it a point to associate with people who are positive and encouraging; you will see your whole world will take on a completely different feeling. When you choose to surround yourself with positive, purposeful, passionate, and productive people you will find yourself cultivating those same empowering qualities.

Mind: My relationships are supportive and empowering.

Body: Take a deep breath. Count "one" to yourself as you exhale. Repeat count with "two" and repeat until you reach count "five."

Spirit: 1 Corinthians 15:33 "Do not be misled: Bad company corrupts good character."

Prayer: Lord help me create healthy boundaries that are wise and godly. Help me to see how my choices of people and relationships can have influences in my life. I pray that people no longer filter my heart and mind. I pray for healthy relationships around me that bring purpose, power, and prayer. Amen.

60 day dose to finding your SPARK....Mind, Body, & Spirit

Day Forty-Five

Reinvent U Daily Vitamin:
Don't Let Others Determine Your Self Worth

How often do we use our mental energy thinking about the acceptance of others? The beauty of who we are lies within our vulnerability, our complex emotions, and our authentic imperfections. Don't change so people will like you, keep being your amazing self and the RIGHT people will love the REAL you. You are more powerful, more worthy, and much greater!! Don't let others determine your worth.

Mind: People do not determine my self-worth.

Body: Lie on your back in bed with a pillow under your head and knees. Breathe in through your nose. Let your belly fill with air. Breathe out through your nose. Place one hand on your belly. Place the other hand on your chest. As you breathe in, feel your belly rise. As you breathe out, feel your belly lower. The hand on your belly should move more than the one that's on your chest. Take three fuller, deep breaths. Breathe fully into your belly as it rises and falls with your breath.

Spirit: Psalm 139:13-15 "For you formed my inward parts; you knitted me together in my mother's womb. I praise you, for I am fearfully and wonderfully made. Wonderful are your works; my soul knows it very well. My frame was not hidden from you, when I was being made in secret, intricately woven in the depths of the earth."

Prayer: *Lord, I pray that you* upgrade my vision for the future, so I never need the validation or acceptance of others. Father lead me away from complacency and any temptation to settle for less than what you know is my absolute best. Help me grasp the depth and perfection of your love, so I am powerful and worthy. Amen.

60 day dose to finding your SPARK....Mind, Body, & Spirit

Day Forty-Six

Reinvent U Daily Vitamin: Sit in the Front Row

How many of us actually sit in the front row so we can enjoy every little bit that life has to offer? I dare you to exchange your balcony tickets for a front row seat. This is your life, and you only live it once. Make the investment and make the time to truly experience your own life being in the FRONT row. There's nothing like it.

Mind: I have a front row seat to my life.

Body: Close your eyes. Take a few big, deep breaths. Breathe in. Imagine that the air is filled with a sense of peace and calm. Try to feel it throughout your body. Breathe out. Now, imagine that the air leaves with your stress and tension. Now use a word or phrase with your breath. As you breathe in, say in your mind, "I breathe in peace and calm." As you breathe out, say in your mind, "I breathe out stress and tension." Continue for 10 to 20 minutes.

Spirit: Psalm 16:11 "You make known to me the path of life; in your presence there is fullness of joy; at your right hand are pleasures forevermore."

Prayer: Lord I pray that you reshape how I think and transform me by the renewing of my mind. I know life is meant to be celebrated, enjoyed, delighted in, and embraced in all its mystery. I pray that I continue to walk down the path that embraces the beauty that surrounds me. Amen.

60 day dose to finding your SPARK....Mind, Body, & Spirit

Day Forty-Seven

Reinvent U Daily Vitamin: Just Be You!!

When you spend too much time concentrating on everyone's perception of you, or who everyone else wants you to be, you eventually forget who you truly are. So don't fear the judgments of others; you know in your heart who you are and what's true to you. You don't have to be someone else to impress people. Let these people be impressed by who you really are!!! Always remember, you were fearfully and wonderfully made.

Mind: I am fearfully and wonderfully made.

Body: Breathe in slowly through your nose, allowing your chest and lower belly to rise as you fill your lungs. Let your abdomen expand fully. Now breathe out slowly through your mouth.

Spirit: Psalm 139:14 "I praise you because I am fearfully and wonderfully made; your works are wonderful, I know that full well."

Prayer: Lord thank you for forming and molding me in your image. Thank you for allowing me to be just me. Thank you for being the master craftsman and creating such masterpiece in me. Amen

60 day dose to finding your SPARK....Mind, Body, & Spirit

Day Forty-Eight

Reinvent U Daily Vitamin: Differences

Many of us grow up feeling dislike or shame related to our differences, and some of us carry that shame into adulthood. Your differences make you outrageously beautiful. Embrace and love your differences and let's challenge ourselves to work on breaking down stigmas, motivating positive perspectives, seeing the ability in all, and respecting and appreciating the value in everyone.

Mind: I love and embrace my differences.

Body: Lie down on your back. Start breathing and observe your chest and stomach move up and down. Continue breathing, but make your breaths deeper and deeper for each inhalation and exhalation.

Spirit: Galatians 3:26 "For in Christ Jesus you are all sons of God, through faith."

Prayer: Lord thank you for showing me how to love my difference and the differences of others. Thank you for allowing me to enjoy the diversity of perspectives, insights, and emotional wiring in others. Amen.

60 day dose to finding your SPARK....Mind, Body, & Spirit

Day: Forty-Nine

Reinvent U Daily Vitamin: Just SMILE!!

Do you know that smiling reduces the stress that your body and mind feel, almost similar to getting good sleep? Studies show women who smiled the most lived happier lives, had happier marriages and had fewer setbacks. A smile can work wonders on your emotional and physical well-being. Always remember smiles are contagious so SMILE, SMILE, SMILE.

Mind: My smile is magnetic.

Body: Sit in a comfortable position and inhale completely. Hold your stomach muscles in completely, while you exhale. Repeat the same for 30 seconds and come back to normal breathing for 3 seconds. Repeat three times.

Spirit: Proverbs 15:13-14 "A glad heart makes a cheerful face, but by sorrow of heart the spirit is crushed. The heart of him who has understanding seeks knowledge, but the mouths of fools feed on folly."

Prayer: Lord thank you for creating me and for the details you put in my design, such as my smile. Thank you for teaching me how to smile more so others can be captivated by my joy. Thank you for giving me a cheerful heart. Amen.

60 day dose to finding your SPARK....Mind, Body, & Spirit

Day Fifty

Reinvent U Daily Vitamin: Get Unstuck

Don't get stuck in the comfort zone of other people. There are people who will suck you into their insecurities in an effort to keep you bound. It's time to get unstuck. It's time to break loose of those chains. It's time to spread your wings and fly! I dare you to stretch your arms forth and reach for your potential, your purpose and your passion. Your BEST is YET to COME!!!

Mind: I am ready to receive and become unstuck

Body: Place your hands on your thighs, lower belly, or you can raise them up into the air in a V-shape over your head. Take a deep breath in through your nose. Forcefully, press your belly button toward your spine as you expel the air from your lungs, breathing out your nose.

Spirit: Romans 8:28 "And we know that in all things God works for the good of those who love him, who have been called according to his purpose."

Prayer: Lord forgive us for allowing circumstances to dictate the attitude of our hearts and to be the focus of our attention. Give us the courage to change what we can change and the strength to break free from the chains that keep us stuck. Thank you for your peace. Amen.

60 day dose to finding your SPARK....Mind, Body, & Spirit

Day Fifty-One

Reinvent U Daily Vitamin: Saving People

I was the queen of trying to save people. This was by far one of the many hard lessons that took me years to learn. The truth is we can't fix people; people fix themselves. We can provide them with the tools they need, but we must learn to step away and allow them to make their own choices. We must have faith in the unfolding of life, and that means letting people have their own experience and believing it is right for their growth.

Mind: Those around me fix themselves.

Body: Close your eyes and breathe naturally for a moment. As you do so, acknowledge your slowing pulse, become aware of how still your mind and body are, and absorb your connection to your entire being. Deepen your breath, inhaling the breath from your belly into your chest. Feel the strength of your life force. Exhale slowly and completely through your nostrils, being patient with your release.

Spirit: Luke 6:38 "Give, and it will be given to you. A good measure, pressed down, shaken together and running over, will be poured into your lap. For with the measure you use, it will be measured to you."

Prayer: Lord I am willing. My heart is surrendered to you, and I want to live as you wish for me to live. Guide me, protect me, and show me what you want me to do, and how to do it. Give me the strength to let go so others can have their own experience and grow. Amen.

60 day dose to finding your SPARK....Mind, Body, & Spirit

Day Fifty-Two

Reinvent U Daily Vitamin:
Don't Worry Be Happy!!

Do you know that worrying saps your time, your energy and your happiness? Worry can have a substantial influence on your wellbeing, creating feelings of apprehension, stress, and anxiety. What can you do to change this? There is a famous song that tells you exactly what to do:

"In your life expect some trouble. But when you worry you make it double. Don't worry, be happy……Don't worry don't do it, be happy. Put a smile on your face."

Do things that make you happy, surround yourself with people that make you happy and more importantly make the choice to be happy, despite……

Mind: My happy thoughts bring happiness into my life.

Body: Sit comfortably, with your spine straight and close your eyes. Use your right thumb and ring finger to alternately block one nostril so you can only breathe through the other nostril. Start by exhaling out the left nostril, and then breathe in through the same nostril. Switch sides after each inhalation. Breathe normally at your own relaxed pace, giving some attention to completing the exhalation, without forcing it.

Spirit: Psalm 37: 4 "Take delight in the LORD, and he will give you the desires of your heart."

Prayer: Lord please help me to rest in your happiness and allow a smile to linger on my lips. Let me have peace in my heart and faith to know that I can cast all my cares on you. Lord, thank you for the smile and thank you for the people in my life that make me smile. Amen.

60 day dose to finding your SPARK....Mind, Body, & Spirit

Day Fifty-Three

Reinvent U Daily Vitamin: AWESOMENESS!!

There was a time in my life, I used to be afraid of doing things because of what others might think or say about me. I was worried about their acceptance and didn't realize the power of this unhealthy behavior. I had to dig deep and find the root cause of my behavior and when I did….I made the choice to be the best me for me, not for others. I was no longer afraid or needed anyone's permission to be awesome. When you are able to consistently see the best in you, you remove the shackles of control to experience a sense of freedom in being your best version of AWESOMENESS.

Mind: I am AWESOME.

Body: Close your eyes and focus all your awareness on your nose. Breathe in and out naturally through your nostrils, and feel each inhalation and exhalation as it passes in or out. Don't count your breaths, don't hold your breath, don't try to breathe any slower, or faster, or deeper than normal. Just be mindful in this moment.

Spirit: Psalm 119: 73-74 "Your hands made me and formed me; give me understanding to learn your commands. May those who fear you rejoice when they see me, for I have put my hope in your word."

Prayer: Lord allow me to keep my heart and thoughts pure and undivided. Protect me from my own careless behaviors, so I am able to remove the shackles that prevent me from being awesome. Amen.

60 day dose to finding your SPARK....Mind, Body, & Spirit

Day Fifty-Four

Reinvent U Daily Vitamin: Be the writer, not the reader!!

Don't be so content reading other people's success story. Start writing your own story and bring success to life. If you want your life story to soar to new heights, you've got to get focused, get rid of the energy vampires who will suck the life out of you, and work diligently to achieve your personal goals. There is absolutely nothing you can't accomplish, so let's get started and get to writing!!

Mind: I own the rights to my story.

Body: Starting with your face, knit your eyebrows together and purse your lips. Try to pull your facial muscles toward your nose for 15-20 seconds and release.

Spirit: Isiah 41:10 "So do not fear, for I am with you; do not be dismayed, for I am your God. I will strengthen you and help you; I will uphold you with my righteous right hand."

Prayer: Lord enlarge my territory and give me the wisdom to spread my wings and fly in the direction of success. Help me Lord to remain focused and humble. Allow me to be the writer and not the reader. Amen.

60 day dose to finding your SPARK....Mind, Body, & Spirit

Day Fifty-Five

Reinvent U Daily Vitamin: Change

All of us will experience metamorphosis several times during our lives, exchanging one identity for another. As you discover more about who you are and what you want out of life, you will find yourself making deliberate changes to keep up with what is happening around you and within you. It will be scary at times but don't allow the fear of change to stop you from taking action. Life only moves in one direction-forward, so embrace the change (s) you need to make and remember change is what prompts personal growth.

Mind: Change helps me grow.

Body: Stand with one leg forward and the other back. Slowly inhale for 3 seconds while lifting your arms above your head. Exhale slowly.

Spirit: 1 Corinthians 4:16-18 "Herefore we do not lose heart. Though outwardly we are wasting away, yet inwardly we are being renewed day by day. For our light and momentary troubles are achieving for us an eternal glory that far outweighs them all. So we fix our eyes not on what is seen, but on what is unseen, since what is seen is temporary, but what is unseen is eternal."

Prayer: Lord help me to not fear change, but embrace it as I embrace you daily. Lord, I trust that you will give me the strength to rise above my fear of change and you will work my life out according to your will and plan. Amen.

60 day dose to finding your SPARK….Mind, Body, & Spirit

Day Fifty-Six

Reinvent U Daily Vitamin: Distractions

We live distracted lives, and our ability to focus, create, and accomplish is impacted significantly. It is our responsibility to live attentive and intentional lives in a world of distractions. Here is my challenge to you, whatever your distraction is, commit to one full week without it. No phone, social media, emails, TV shows, and people, etc,. When distractions are eliminated, you will find yourself with plenty of space to explore new things and focus on what really matters.

Mind: I am focused on what matters.

Body: Focus on the sensation of air flowing into your nostrils and out of your mouth. Become aware of sounds, sensations, and thoughts. Embrace and consider each thought or sensation without judging it good or bad. If your mind starts to race, return your focus to your breathing. Then expand your awareness again.

Spirit: Proverbs 4:25 "Let your eyes look straight ahead; fix your gaze directly before you."

Prayer: Lord I refuse to allow the distractions of this world to hinder my focus, creativity, and accomplishments. Reveal those things Lord that needs to be eliminated from my life. Thank you for space to explore new things and focus on what really matters. Amen.

60 day dose to finding your SPARK....Mind, Body, & Spirit

Day Fifty-Seven

Reinvent U Daily Vitamin: No Judgement

Let's work on paying attention to the thoughts we have of others and understand that people are doing the best that they can to respond to their experience. The sooner we start to recognize our judgmental behaviors and discover the true reasons behind them, the sooner we can deal with them and work on letting them go.

Mind: I release the need to judge others

Body: From a standing position, bend forward from the waist with your knees slightly bent, letting your arms dangle close to the floor. As you inhale slowly and deeply, return to a standing position by rolling up slowing, lifting your head last. Hold your breath for just a few seconds in this standing position.

Spirit: Matthew 7:1-2 "Do not judge, or you too will be judged. For in the same way you judge others, you will be judged, and with the measure you use, it will be measured to you."

Prayer: Lord I repent from judging others or having judgmental thoughts. Lord, I choose to walk in love and forgiveness and submit my thoughts to you. Teach me how to pray for others and give me an abundance of compassion and mercy. Lord bless those that I have judged in the past. Amen.

60 day dose to finding your SPARK....Mind, Body, & Spirit

Day Fifty-Eight

Reinvent U Daily Vitamin: P-A-T-I-E-N-C-E

How many of us hate to hear the word "PATIENCE"? When we think of patience, we think of waiting. And most of us don't like to wait. The truth is we can't have patience without the waiting. But here is an important fact: if we want to grow, be successful and achieve your goals you must put the work in and practice patience. Think about this, if you plant a seed, water it, leave it for some time, then at the right time, when all the right elements are in place that seed turns into a flower. You see, the seed had to be planted, it had to be nurtured; it had to be left alone so the roots can grow under the soil and when ALL the elements were RIGHT, it began to rise above the surface into exactly what it was meant to be. Work and patience was a part of the flowers growth process. So keep putting in the work and cultivating patience……your flower is coming.

Mind: I believe patience is a powerful virtue.

Body: Take a deep breath through your nose as you count to three. Exhale through your mouth counting to five. After ten breaths, take a few big deep inhalations and exhalations and resume breathing normally for a minute or so.

Spirit: Colossians 1:11 "being strengthened with all power according to his glorious might so that you may have great endurance and patience,"

Prayer: Lord teach me to be patient with my life, family, friends, coworkers, and more importantly with myself. Teach me to trust in you and your timing rather than leaning on my own understanding. Help me to put the work in to cultivate patience so I can embrace the flower that is slowly blooming. Amen.

60 day dose to finding your SPARK....Mind, Body, & Spirit

Day Fifty-Nine

Reinvent U Daily Vitamin: Choose to Love

Love has a different meaning and feeling to each individual person. Love is universal across every culture and language around the world, and it's also a very powerful emotion. Love has been shown to have healing properties. Holistic medicine firmly follows the idea that love has strong healing powers. Studies have shown that people who have someone to love or have someone who loves them, live longer than those who do not. Let's hit that love button and choose to love!!

Mind: I give and receive love.

Body: Lie on your back and begin to observe your breath just as it is. Notice where the breath flows; upper chest, lower belly, front, back, or sides. You will notice that as you observe your breath, it will slow down your respiration rate.

Spirit: 1 Corinthians 13:4-8 "Love is patient, love is kind. It does not envy, it does not boast, it is not proud. It does not dishonor others, it is not self-seeking, it is not easily angered, it keeps no record of wrongs. Love does not delight in evil but rejoices with the truth. It always protects, always trusts, always hopes, always perseveres. Love never fails."

Prayer: Lord thank you for your never failing and never-ending love, grace, and faithfulness. May I continue to be an example of love and I pray that your perfect love surrounds me every day of my life. Amen.

60 day dose to finding your SPARK....Mind, Body, & Spirit

Day Sixty

Reinvent U Daily Vitamin: A NEW Ending

I recently saw this quote, "No one can go back and start a new beginning, but anyone can start today and make a new ending" (Unknown). Every day you wake up you have yet another chance to make it right. To start making positive changes within us, to start taking chances in life, to start working on our BIG dreams, to start living fearlessly. Let's create a NEW ending to our book of life.

Mind: I am creating a new ending in my book of life.

Body: Close your eyes and take a deep breath through your nose, count to 4 and release slowly through your mouth. Breathe normal and repeat the deep breathing after 30 seconds.

Spirit: Isaiah 43:19 "Forget the former things; do not dwell on the past. See, I am doing a new thing! Now it springs up; do you not perceive it? I am making a way in the wilderness and streams in the wasteland."

Prayer: Lord draw me closer to you so I can be fearless in creating a new ending in my book of life. Be with me Lord with each passing day so as you lead, I follow and as you teach I learn. I pray that as I take my daily dose of vitamins my souls in enriched, my body is strengthened and my mind is renewed. Thank you for giving me the chance to live, love and dream big. Amen.

60 day dose to finding your SPARK….Mind, Body, & Spirit

About The Author

Ms. Cuesta is a sought-after expert on loss and life. As a certified life coach specializing in trauma healing, she travels the region helping women rebuild their lives after personal tragedies and loss. Known for her authenticity and straight-from-the-hip approach, Frances's passion is fueled by her own pursuit of happiness and freedom. The personal challenges she has faced once seemed insurmountable. She has loved and lost. She has been beaten and broken. A domestic violence survivor, she has stared death in the face. But God had a different ending for her story. Today, she shares the unedited narrative of her life, inspiring others to redefine their own. An impassioned speaker, she delivers motivational messages to professional, personal development, women's empowerment and grief/trauma support groups. Ms. Cuesta's diverse educational and professional experiences in the mental health and coaching fields inspire her passion for encouraging, empowering, and equipping women to improve and heal from trauma and loss.

Ms. Cuesta is a Desensitization Counselor who provides direct exposure for individuals experiencing workplace-related Post Traumatic Stress Disorder (PTSD). Frances is also a champion survivor of PTSD and knows the meaning of perseverance and healing. Frances is a volunteer for the American Red Cross Action Disaster Team, and she also provides Critical Incident Stress Management Debriefing (CISM) to various corporations through her company Serenity Healing Institute of Baltimore. Serenity Institute of Baltimore is a for-profit organization that provides women, men, and businesses affected by trauma with high-quality holistic healing services. Ms. Cuesta is also the founder and CEO of Reinvent U Boot Camps, LLC; a group fitness facility that provides a supportive environment where women can enjoy a variety of fun and diverse fitness classes while achieving their weight loss and fitness goals. At Reinvent U Boot Camps, the focus is on women "Losing Weight from the Inside Out" to adopt sustainable lifestyle changes that enhance their health and vitality.

Ms. Cuesta's leisure pursuits include personal fitness workouts, Latin dancing, and cooking. Ms. Cuesta is married with two adult children and one precious granddaughter.

Contact Information:

Reinvent U Boot Camps LLC
1321A Bedford Avenue
Pikesville, MD 21208
410-602-UFIT
www.reinventubootcamps.com

Serenity Healing Institute Of Baltimore LLC
1321A Bedford Avenue
Pikesville, MD 21208
410-602- 8348
www.serenityhealinginstituteofbaltimore.org

www.ingramcontent.com/pod-product-compliance
Lightning Source LLC
Chambersburg PA
CBHW070613010526
44118CB00012B/1499